First Facts

The LIFE and TIMES of
Pocahontas
and the First Colonies

by Marissa Kirkman

CAPSTONE PRESS
a capstone imprint

First Facts are published by Capstone Press,
1710 Roe Crest Drive, North Mankato, Minnesota 56003
www.mycapstone.com

Library of Congress Cataloging-in-Publication Data
Names: Kirkman, Marissa, author.
Title: The life and times of Pocahontas and the first colonies / by Marissa
    Kirkman.
Description: North Mankato, Minnesota : Capstone Press, [2017] | Series:
    First facts. Life and times | Includes bibliographical references and
    index. | Audience: Ages 7–9.
Identifiers: LCCN 2016009011| ISBN 9781515724773 (library binding) |
    ISBN 9781515724858 (pbk.) | ISBN 9781515724896 (ebook pdf)
Subjects: LCSH: Pocahontas, –1617—Juvenile literature. | Powhatan
    women—Biography—Juvenile literature. | Jamestown
    (Va.)—History—Juvenile literature.
Classification: LCC E99.P85 K58 2017 | DDC 975.501092—dc23
LC record available at http://lccn.loc.gov/2016009011

Editorial Credits
Charmaine Whitman, designer; Tracy Cummins, media researcher;
Tori Abraham, production specialist

Image Credits
Bridgeman Images: Private Collection, Cover Left; Capstone Press: Mapping
Specialists, 5; Getty Images: Hulton Archive, 11, MPI, 13, 15, Stock
Montage, 16, Time Life Pictures/Mansell, 9; Granger NYC: 17; iStockphoto:
HultonArchive, 6; Library of Congress: Cover Right, 1, 21; North Wind
Picture Archives: 7, 19; Shutterstock: Apostrophe, Design Elements

Table of Contents

Before the United States

Before the United States was a country, Native Americans lived on the land. They lived in groups called **tribes**. Many different tribes had been living across North America for hundreds of years. In the early 1600s, the Powhatan **Confederacy** was a group of 30 tribes. This group was led by Chief Powhatan. They lived in what is now the U.S. state of Virginia.

---

tribe—a group of people who share the same ancestors, customs, and laws

confederacy—a union of people or groups with a common goal

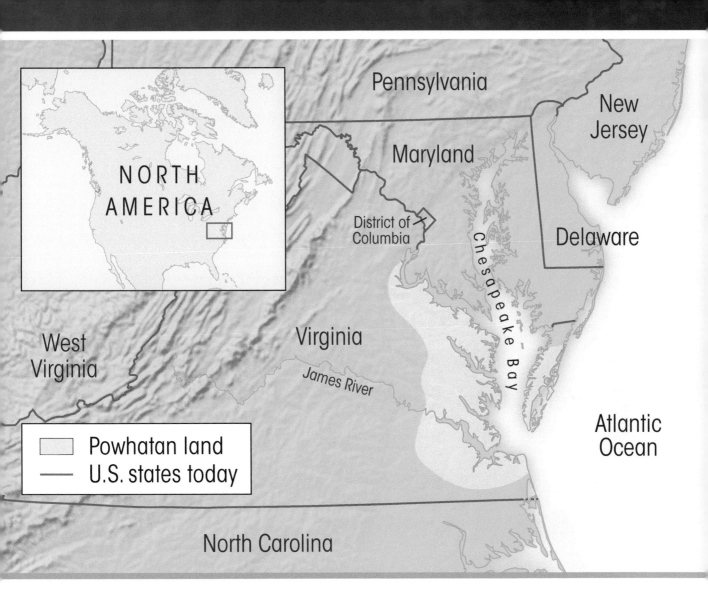

NORTH AMERICA

Pennsylvania

New Jersey

Maryland

District of Columbia

Chesapeake Bay

Delaware

West Virginia

Virginia

James River

Atlantic Ocean

Powhatan land
— U.S. states today

North Carolina

Fact: Each of the 30 tribes in the Powhatan Confederacy had its own chief. All of those chiefs followed Chief Powhatan.

Pocahontas was Chief Powhatan's daughter. She was born around 1595. Her given name was Matoaka. Pocahontas was her **nickname**. Young Powhatan girls, such as Pocahontas, helped to build homes and take care of younger children. They also helped grow food, such as squash, corn, and beans. Powhatan men built **canoes** to fish in the rivers.

Fact: Pocahontas's nickname means "Little Wanton," or little spirited one. Some historians believe that Pocahontas got her nickname because she was very curious.

nickname—a name used with or instead of a real name

canoe—a small, shallow boat that people move through water with paddles

Colonists Arrive

When Pocahontas was about 12 years old, things changed for the Powhatans. In 1607 men from England traveled in large ships to start a **colony**. The **colonists** named their new town Jamestown, after King James I. Many colonists hoped to find gold and become rich. They did not know that the Powhatans already lived on this land.

colony—an area that has been settled by people from another country

colonist—a person who lives in a colony

Fact: King James I sent men to America in three ships named *Discovery*, *Godspeed*, and *Susan Constant*.

Building a Home

Once on land, the colonists built **shelters**. They also built a **fort** with tall walls to keep their shelters safe inside. They called it Fort James. Building the fort was hard work. Most of the colonists did not know how to build. Many colonists had been rich in England. They were used to having other people do jobs for them.

Fact: The Jamestown colonists built their fort on damp, swampy land with lots of bugs. The water was too salty, and it made them sick.

shelter—a safe, covered place

fort—a place built to be strong to keep the people living there safe from attack

Hard Times

Many colonists did not know how to hunt, fish, or grow their own food. Nearby tribes saw the colonists making a new home on the land. They became angry that the colonists were taking over native land. The two groups began to fight. Because of the fighting, the colonists were afraid to hunt for food.

Fact: The colonists also went hungry because they did not know which plants were safe to eat. Many colonists died because they were sick or hungry.

Trading Partners

Not all tribes were angry with the colonists. Chief Powhatan learned that the colonists were hungry. He sent some of his people, along with Pocahontas, to bring them food. The Powhatans **traded** with the colonists. They gave the colonists food and the colonists gave them **copper** and tools. Pocahontas returned to Jamestown many times. The colonists felt that Pocahontas saved them by bringing food.

Fact: As the chief's daughter, Pocahontas often joined Chief Powhatan when he met important people. Colonists thought of Pocahontas as a Native American princess.

trade—to exchange one item for another

copper—a reddish brown metal

Pocahontas and John Smith

Pocahontas visited the colonists many times. She brought them food to trade for things her tribe needed. She brought messages from her father. Pocahontas met John Smith when she visited Jamestown. He was a leader of the colonists. Pocahontas and John Smith became friends. A big fire burned most of Jamestown in 1608. After the fire, Pocahontas brought food to the colonists and Smith.

Fact: Some stories say that Pocahontas saved John Smith's life. Many historians say this did not happen.

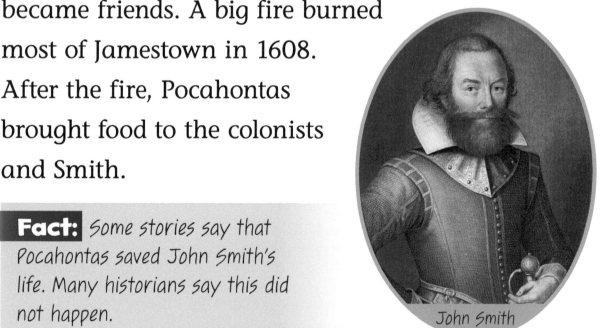
John Smith

Pocahontas brought food to the colonists.

More Colonists Arrive

In January 1608 another ship arrived with more colonists, food, and **supplies.** More ships came the next year. With more and more colonists living in Jamestown, they used more land to build homes. Jamestown was growing. Some tribes did not like that the colonists were taking over the land. They did not want to lose their native lands. The two sides fought over the land.

Fact: John Smith went back to England in October 1609.

supplies—materials needed to do something

A Friendship Ends

As Jamestown grew larger, Chief Powhatan understood the colonists were not leaving. He didn't want to help them anymore. They were taking his land. He stopped trading with them. The colonists were upset because they needed to trade for food. Over the next few years the colonists and many tribes fought many times. In 1613 the colonists took Pocahontas, hoping to trade her for food and **weapons**.

Fact: Pocahontas was not returned to her tribe. Instead, she became a colonist. Her name was changed to Rebecca.

weapon—something used to injure or harm

peace—a time without war or fighting

An Important Woman

When she was about 19, Pocahontas married colonist John Rolfe. After they were married there was very little fighting for a while. This time was called the **Peace** of Pocahontas. Pocahontas and her husband went to England to meet the king and queen. They hoped this meeting would help England respect the Powhatan people. On their way home, Pocahontas became sick and died. She is remembered as an important person who helped the early colonists.

Glossary

canoe (kuh-NOO)—a small, shallow boat that people move through water with paddles

colonist (KAH-luh-nist)—a person who lives in a colony

colony (KAH-luh-nee)—an area that has been settled by people from another country

confederacy (kuhn-FED-ur-uh-see)—a union of people or groups with a common goal

copper (KAH-pur)—a reddish brown metal

fort (FORT)—a place built to be strong to keep the people living there safe from attack

nickname (NIK-name)—a name used with or instead of a real name

peace (PEES)—a time without war or fighting

shelter (SHEL-tur)—a safe, covered place

supplies (suh-PLIZE)—materials needed to do something

trade (TRADE)—to exchange one item for another

tribe (TRIBE)—a group of people who share the same ancestors, customs, and laws

weapon (WEP-uhn)—something used to injure or harm

Read More

Edison, Erin. *Pocahontas.* Great Women in History. North Mankato, MN: Capstone Press, 2013.

Levy, Janey. *Life in Jamestown Colony.* What You Didn't Know About History. New York: Gareth Stevens Publishing, 2014.

Smith, Andrea P. *Pocahontas and John Smith.* Jr. Graphic Colonial America. New York: PowerKids Press, 2012.

Internet Sites

FactHound offers a safe, fun way to find Internet sites related to this book. All of the sites on FactHound have been researched by our staff.

Here's all you do:

Visit *www.facthound.com*

Type in this code: 9781515724773

Super-cool stuff!

Check out projects, games and lots more at
www.capstonekids.com

Critical Thinking Using the Common Core

1. In what ways did Pocahontas help the Jamestown colonists? (Key Ideas and Details)

2. What is the author telling you in the Fact box on page 10? (Craft and Structure)

Index